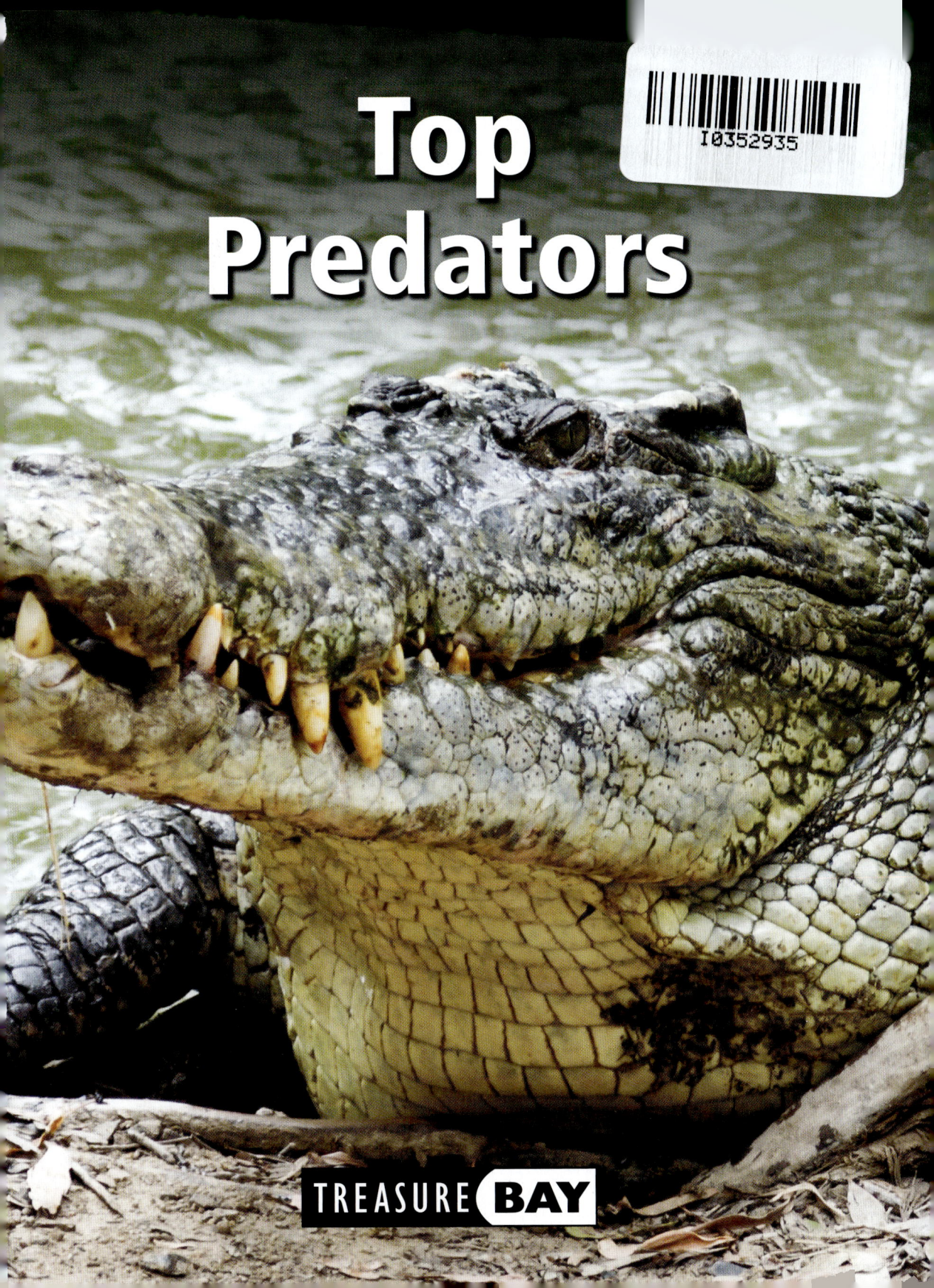

WE BOTH READ®

Introduction
Top Predators

We Both Read books are perfect to read with a buddy—or to read by yourself! If you are reading the book alone, you can read it like any other book. If you are reading with another person, you can take turns reading aloud. When taking turns, it's usually a good idea  for the reader with more experience to read the more difficult parts, marked with a blue dot ●. The reader with somewhat less experience can read the parts marked with a red star ★.

Sharing the reading of a book can be a lot of fun, and reading aloud is a great way to improve fluency and expression. If you are reading with someone else, you might also  want to take the time to talk about what you are reading and what else you would like to know about these top predators. After reading with someone else, you might even want to experience reading the entire book on your own.

Top Predators

A We Both Read® Chapter Book
Level 3
Blue dot text—Guided Reading Level: S
Red star text—Guided Reading Level: Q

With special thanks to Emma Kocina, Biologist
at the California Academy of Sciences for her
review of the information in this book

Text Copyright © 2025 by Sindy McKay
Use of photographs provided by iStock, Dreamstime, and Shutterstock.

All rights reserved

We Both Read® is a trademark of Treasure Bay, Inc.

Published by
Treasure Bay, Inc.
PO Box 519
Roseville, CA 95661 USA

Printed in China

Library of Congress Control Number: 2024909716

ISBN: 978-1-60115-380-7

Visit us online at:
WeBothRead.com

PR-11-24

Table of Contents

Chapter 1
Top Predators 2

Chapter 2
How to Be a Top Predator 6

Chapter 3
Predators on Land 16

Chapter 4
Birds of Prey 22

Chapter 5
Aquatic Predators 28

Chapter 6
The Only Enemy: Humans 34

Glossary 42

Questions to Ask After Reading 43

CHAPTER 1   TOP PREDATORS

Owl

Great white shark

- A predator is any animal that hunts down, kills, and eats other animals. Many predators appear frightening with their big teeth, sharp claws, and powerful jaws.

   There are many species of predators in the animal kingdom, and many of them are also prey. For example, rats eat grasshoppers, but a rat may then be hunted, killed, and eaten by a fox. The fox may then become dinner for a bear. Bears, however, are not preyed upon by any other animal. This classifies them as a top predator. A top predator is one that, when full-grown and healthy, is not hunted by any other animal in their natural **environment**.

Gray wolf

Grizzly bear

Lion

⭐ **Environment** is extremely important in determining a top predator's success. A lion would not last long in the Arctic cold while a polar bear is not built to thrive on the plains of Africa. A killer whale may rule in the ocean but would not survive in the trees of a tropical rain forest.

There can, however, be more than one top predator in a specific environment. For example, sperm whales and killer whales are both excellent hunters with no natural enemies in the same ocean waters. Bobcats and wolves are both on top in the forests of the United States.

Killer whale

- The hunting and eating of other animals may seem cruel, but predators play an extremely important role in keeping animal populations in balance to maintain a healthy ecosystem.

A simple way to explain an ecosystem is through the food chain.

The first link in the food chain is plants.

The next link is the animals that only consume plants, such as giraffes, deer, and bugs.

Predators, or meat-eaters, are next in the chain.

These meat-eaters may then be eaten by other meat-eaters.

The animals at the very top of the food chain are called **apex** predators. They have no natural enemies. Their population is controlled through competition for resources and the natural aging process.

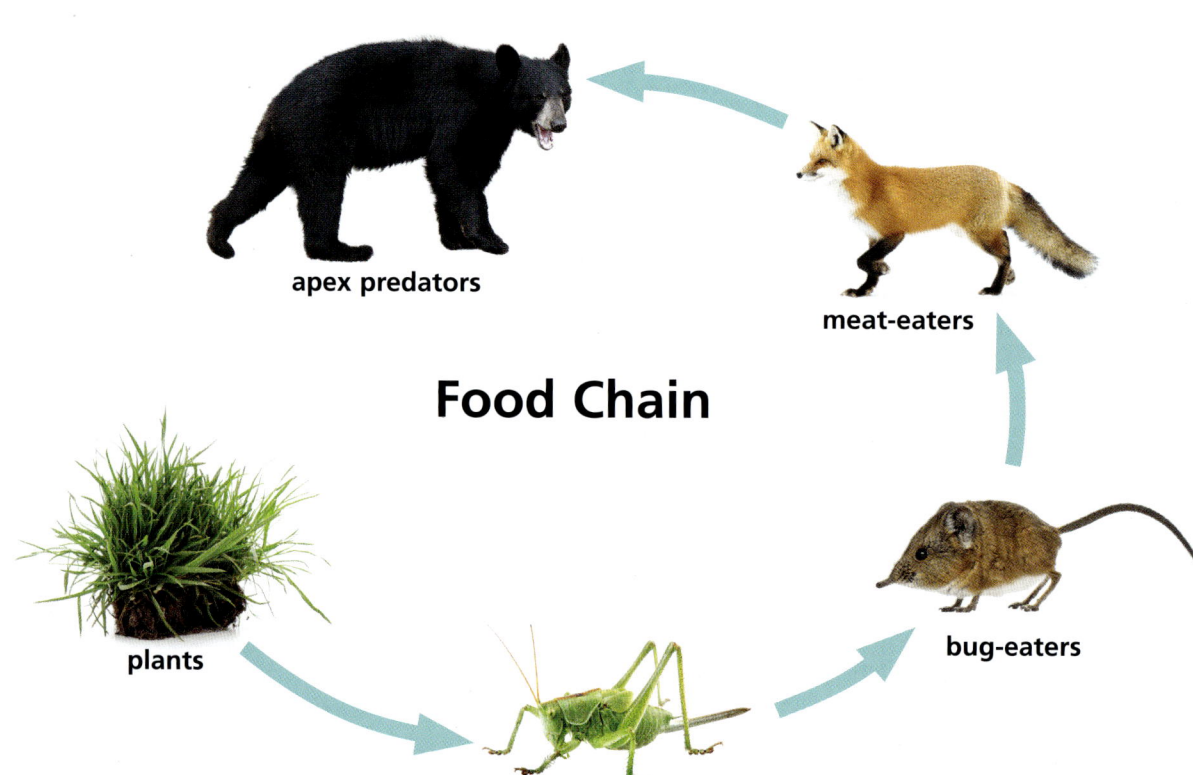

Food Chain

apex predators

meat-eaters

bug-eaters

plant-eaters

plants

Leopard   Baboons

★   The health of an ecosystem requires a delicate balance. **Apex** predators are an essential part of that balance. When an apex predator is removed, serious problems may occur.

When leopards in parts of Africa were almost wiped out, the baboon population exploded. The baboons attacked livestock, damaged crops, and spread parasites to humans.

Sea otters were once almost wiped out by hunters. Otters eat sea urchins. Without otters, urchins thrived. The urchins began to destroy ocean kelp forests. Kelp forests are an important habitat for many sea animals. Fortunately, people are now helping otters make a comeback.

Kelp forest

Sea otter

CHAPTER 2
HOW TO BE A TOP PREDATOR

Malayan tiger

Siberian tiger

- Top predators earn their position in nature in many ways. One quality found in many apex hunters is stealth, which is the ability to sneak up quietly on your prey before going in for the kill.

    Cats are renowned for their stealth, and tigers are true masters. Their excellent vision and hearing allow them to hunt in low light when their striped coat provides a form of camouflage in the shadows. They silently stalk an unsuspecting victim, then pounce on its back, biting its neck and often breaking its spinal cord.

    Spiders may be small compared to other apex predators, but when it comes to being sneaky, the trapdoor spider is one of the best. These spiders live in underground **burrows**.

Trapdoor spider

Trapdoor spider  | Barn owl

⭐ These spiders build a hinged cover on top of their **burrow**. They wait for prey to walk past. Then they pop up out of the "trapdoor," grab the prey, and bite. The spider's fangs deliver venom that turns the prey's insides into mush, which the spider then eats.

Owls are another animal that uses stealth, swooping quietly down on victims from the sky. With special feathers that absorb much of the noise of flight, they can fly just inches from their prey with barely a sound. Once an owl has its prey in its powerful claws there is no escape.

Eurasion eagle-owl foot | Little owl

Cheetah

- Speed is another advantage for some predators. Cheetahs have been known to run at speeds up to 75 miles an hour—faster than cars are allowed to go on most highways. However, cheetahs can only run at this **exceptional** speed in short bursts, so stealth must also be used. A cheetah will creep up slowly on its prey before taking chase and pouncing.

  The fastest predatory animal ever recorded is the peregrine falcon. They have been clocked reaching speeds of 240 miles per hour while diving for prey—faster than a small airplane! Falcons have an aerodynamic torso that reduces the drag from air moving past at high speeds. Their specially pointed wings can beat up to four times per second while they are in flight.

Peregrine falcon

Bald eagle

★ Many apex predators also have excellent eyes. Eagles can spot prey up to two miles away. But they do not see as well in the dark.

Owls, on the other hand, can see any time of the day or night! Great eyes plus their ability to fly silently makes them **exceptional** hunters. Mice and other prey on the ground never know they're coming until it's too late.

Tawny owl

Brown bear

- A strong sense of smell helps some predators sniff out their prey from great distances. Most zoologists agree that bears have the best sense of smell of any animal on earth. A bear's sense of smell is over 2,000 times better than a human's. It can zero in on a source of food from several miles away. This may be why campers in bear country are strongly urged to keep their food in extra strong food containers placed at least 100 feet downwind of their campsite.

Great white shark

★ Sharks have such a remarkable sense of smell that sometimes they are called "swimming noses." A great white shark can smell blood in the water at about one part per 10 billion parts water. This ability helps them track and hunt wounded or dying animals.

A great white shark rushes toward its prey, attacking from beneath. They will often jump completely out of the water to grab a seal or other marine mammal.

Anaconda

- Perhaps the best advantage for an apex predator is sheer strength, and few animals demonstrate this better than the green anaconda.

This powerful animal is huge, with an average length of 30 feet and weight of 550 pounds. That makes it as long as a two-story building is high and as heavy as some refrigerators. Native to South America, anaconda hunt on land and in the water.

Using sight and smell to locate prey, it grabs the prey with its mouth and coils itself around the animal's body. The snake then squeezes tightly, so the animal can't take a breath. After the prey suffocates, the snake opens its mouth wide and swallows the meal whole. After a big meal, an anaconda can go for weeks without eating again.

Coconut crab

★ One of the most surprising top predators is the coconut crab. Most crabs are small. This powerful crab can be three feet wide. Coconut crabs spend their early life in the ocean waters. As adults they live only on land. They hunt mostly at night. When a rat passes by, the crab grabs it with a claw. The claw's grip is almost as strong as the bite of a lion.

The crab can climb trees to find birds sleeping in nests. It sneaks up to grab a bird's wing. This breaks the wing, making the bird unable to fly. The crab then drops the bird to the ground, where the crab can easily grab and eat it.

Saltwater crocodile

• With a set of jaws that can apply 3,700 pounds of pressure per square inch, the dangerously aggressive **saltwater crocodile** has the highest bite force of any animal. *Salties*, as they are sometimes called, are found in coastal waters of Australia, New Guinea, and Southeast Asia. They live in both salty sea water and freshwater rivers. Saltwater crocodiles lurk along the water's edge and attack any prey that approaches with a violent lunge. It then pulls the prey underwater and drowns it before bringing it back up to eat above water. If the prey is large, the crocodile will do a "death roll" while underwater, spinning to drown the prey.

Saltwater crocodile

⭐ The **saltwater crocodile** is one of the oldest animal species that is still alive today. There were saltwater crocodiles during the time of the dinosaurs! Males can grow to be more than 23 feet long. They have a mouthful of 66 teeth. If one falls out or breaks, another one will grow to replace it. The larger canine teeth can grow to be five inches long. Most crocodiles do not attack humans, but a saltwater crocodile will lash out to protect its territory.

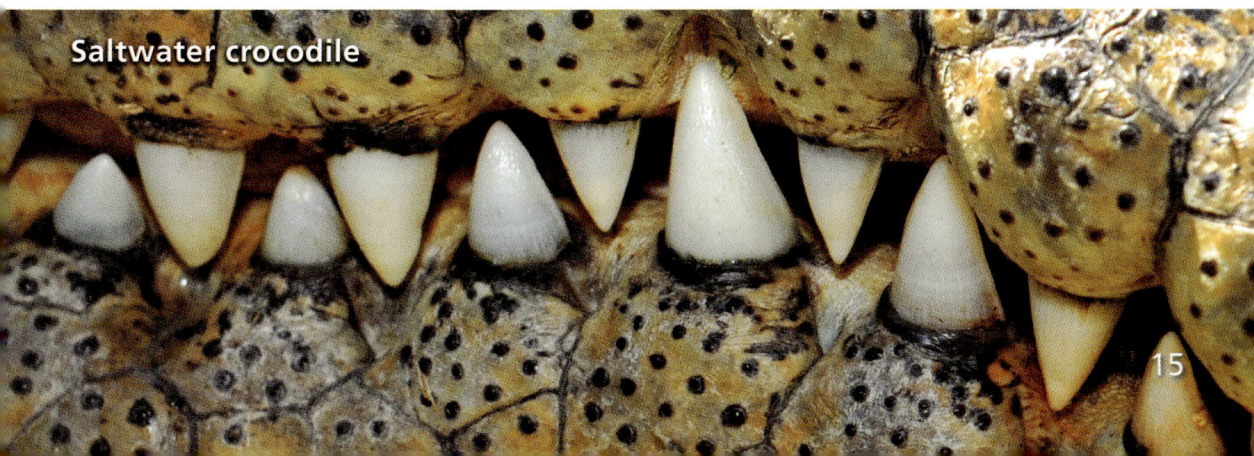

Saltwater crocodile

CHAPTER 3   PREDATORS ON LAND

Lion cub

Lions and Cape buffalo

- On the plains of the Serengeti on the continent of Africa, the lion is king. Females of the pride are the main hunters and usually hunt in small groups. They work together to surround and ambush their prey. The "wing" lions run out to the sides of the intended target. They drive it toward the "center" lion, who is waiting to ambush the prey once it is in position. This lion is usually the largest so it can do the most damage when it pounces on top of the victim.

African buffalo and lion

★ Wolves are another animal that hunts in a pack. A wolf pack will sometimes trail a herd of elk or other large prey for days before making their move. During that time, they are figuring out which herd members are the weakest. The old, young, injured, or slow are the easiest to take down. Weeding out the weaker members of a herd sounds mean, but it actually helps to keep the herd strong. Only the fastest and smartest members will survive to pass their genes on to the next generation.

Gray wolves

Eastern wolves

Snow leopard

Snow leopard cubs

- Many apex predators prefer to hunt alone. One such **solitary** hunter is the snow leopard. Much smaller than a lion, this cat is no less adept at hunting. It can take down animals that are two to four times its own weight. Often referred to as the "ghost of the mountains," this beautiful cat is perfectly adapted to its home high in the snowy mountain ranges of Asia. Like other big cats, it stalks its prey until it is close enough to chase it down. Its big, broad paws act as snowshoes and give it traction as it chases its prey across stones, snow, and icy surfaces. It then leaps from several feet away to land atop the animal and pull it down.

Snow leopard

Grizzly bear

⭐ Grizzly bears are also **solitary** hunters. They are surprisingly fast. They stalk large prey, such as elk, until they get close. Then they chase, pounce, and kill the prey with bites to the spine.

A grizzly's favorite food may be fish. It will stand close to the banks of a river and flip fish out of the water with its large paws. Or it may sit on a rock in deep water. When it spots a fish it will dive in to grab it. Once a year, salmon leap upstream to spawn. Then a grizzly can simply wait for a fish to leap up and into its mouth!

Tasmanian devil

- The only marsupial *(mar-SOOP-ee-el)* to make the list of top predators is the ferocious Tasmanian devil. Marsupials are a type of mammal that gives birth to tiny babies that then continue developing in a pouch outside of their mother's body. The large island of Tasmania may be the last place Tasmanian devils can be found. With the most powerful bite relative to body size of any predatory mammal on Earth, Tasmanian devils have no natural enemies in their native habitat.

  A vital part of the island's ecosystem, Tasmanian devils hunt invasive nonnative species like feral cats and black rats. This helps protect smaller prey animals like bandicoots and possums. Sadly, their population is seriously threatened due to an unusual cancer that only affects Tasmanian devils and has killed off almost 80 percent of these animals.

Tasmanian devils

Polar bear

Polar bear

★ Who is the top "top predator" on land? There is much debate, but many scientists agree that it is the polar bear. The largest of all bear species, they can weigh well over a thousand pounds and stand over 10 feet high.

Seals are their most common prey. They wait next to a hole in the ice for a seal to come to the surface to breathe. Then they bite or grab the seal and pull it onto the ice.

CHAPTER 4   BIRDS OF PREY

Eagle foot with talons

Red-tailed hawk

- Birds of prey, as these apex predators are often called, pursue a variety of animals. They themselves are prey to no other native animals. Birds of prey include eagles, owls, hawks, falcons, and osprey. They are also called raptors, which mean "to seize and carry off." With their sharp nails, called talons, they are able to catch and hold onto animals as large as a coyote. Their sharp beaks allow them to easily eat the prey once it's caught.

Bald eagle

Bald eagle

Red-tailed hawk

⭐ Birds of prey are known for their amazing eyesight. The red-tailed hawk has eyesight that is eight times as powerful as human's. This helps them spot a tiny mouse from one hundred feet above—that's as high as a 10-story building!

While in the air, hawks do something called "kiting." They hover in the air while the wind blows against them. This is much like a kite tugging against its string. Hawks are one of the few birds that do this.

Red-tailed hawk

Red-tailed hawk

Osprey

Osprey

- Many birds of prey hunt primarily fish. The osprey *(AW-spree)* is one such bird. One of the oldest bird species, osprey have been around for millions of years. They can be found in almost every part of the world, as long as there is water nearby. This raptor dives, usually feet first, into shallow water to capture its prey with its **talons**.

    Osprey build their nests near the water, in tall trees or on poles. They continue to add material to their nest every year and some nests can grow up to 10-feet high.

Osprey nest

Osprey family

Amur falcon

Falcon and hare

★ Falcons are beautiful birds, both while in flight and while resting. Like all birds of prey, they have great speed, amazing eyesight, and powerful **talons**. Because of this, falcons are often captured and trained by humans to hunt for them. Sometimes the hunt is for food. Sometimes it is just for sport. Hunting with falcons has been around for more than three thousand years.

Saker falcon

Harris hawks

Harris hawk

- While most raptors are solitary hunters, there are a few exceptions. Harris hawks are known to hunt in packs, earning them the title "wolves of the sky."

Found primarily in the American Southwest, these birds hunt cottontails, jackrabbits, and other small mammals found in desert habitats. Working together, the birds on the ground surround the prey and flush it out of hiding. The prey will run out into the open where other birds are waiting to snatch it up. Another technique has them taking turns chasing the prey, back and forth, until the prey tires and they are able to grab it. Once the prey is caught, the hawks use their sharp and powerful beaks to share the meal with their pack.

Harpy eagle

Harpy eagle feet

★ Which top predator might be considered the "king of the sky"? Many agree it is the harpy eagle. This giant bird can be found high in the treetops of South American rain forests. They dive down from a high perch to grab prey with their strong talons. These talons are the largest of any bird. They can crush the bones of their prey, instantly killing it. Their prey includes sloths, monkeys, and many other animals that are almost as big as the eagle.

Harpy eagle

27

CHAPTER 5   AQUATIC PREDATORS

Great white shark

- Great white sharks are not the largest type of shark, yet they have a reputation as the most dangerous. As an apex predator, they present a clear danger to other animals in the ocean, but attacks on humans are quite rare. Tiger sharks and bull sharks are actually more dangerous to humans as they live in shallow coastal waters where people are more likely to be participating in water sports.

    All of these sharks are top predators with only one enemy in their ocean world—the orca, or killer whale. When a shark catches the scent of an orca it heads off in the other direction!

Sand tiger shark

Killer whale

Piranhas

★ In the water of the Amazon River live the small but mighty piranha *(prr-AH-nah)*. These fish have sharp teeth and strong jaws that can slice through bone. For small prey they may hunt alone. But often they hunt in a pack. A pack may go after very large animals, such as capybaras *(cap-ee-BAR-ahs)*. The pack will swarm the prey and take turns biting big chunks of flesh off it. They have even been known to attack humans when no other prey is available! Luckily, these attacks are rarely fatal.

Piranha

Capybaras

Giant river otter

- When thinking of top predators, otters don't usually come to mind. The giant river otter, however, definitely makes the list. Found primarily in the Amazon region, these creatures can grow up to six feet long and weigh 50 to 70 pounds. They live together in family groups of four to eight, and within the group they are peaceful and cooperative. When it comes to hunting, however, they are ruthless.

   In shallow water they may hunt alone. In deeper water, they hunt in a group. Fast swimmers, they chase their prey underwater, lunging and twisting, until they grab it in their jaws. They then eat it, headfirst, bones and all. Their main prey is fish, but they will also eat frogs, snakes, and the occasional **caiman** *(KAY-min)*.

Giant river otters

Anaconda 　　**Caiman**

⭐　　Giant river otters are just one of the many apex predators in the Amazon. Anaconda snakes, **caiman**, bull sharks, and jaguars are all at the top of the food chain. But this does not mean that they are always safe. If any one of these animals is young, sick, weak, or injured, it may become dinner for the others.

Great white shark 　　**Jaguar**

Electric eel

- One more apex predator found in the waters of South America is the electric eel. Despite their name, they are not eels at all. They are freshwater fish that spends most of their time at the bottom of muddy rivers and streams. Electric eels primarily eat small fish, reptiles, and mammals, which they first immobilize with an electric shock. Depending on the species, this fish can release an electric shock of up to 860 volts. This temporarily paralyzes the prey, and the eel then swallows it whole.

   Electric eels can and do sometimes accidentally electrocute themselves and other eels, but because the shocks they deliver are meant for smaller prey, it's rarely lethal to the eel.

Killer whales

★ Most scientists agree that the top "top predator" of the ocean is the orca. Orcas are often called killer whales, but they are not whales. They are a member of the dolphin family. Orcas are very social animals and travel in groups, called pods. These groups will hunt together, chasing their prey until the prey is too tired to resist. Male adult orcas can consume 100 to 300 pounds of food each day. They most often swallow their food whole. Meals include seals, smaller whales, fish, sharks, turtles, and sea birds.

CHAPTER 6 THE ONLY ENEMY: HUMANS

Polar bear

- It is a sad truth that many top predators are endangered. For some it is due to loss of habitat. As land is cleared for humans to use, the predatory animals' hunting range is narrowed and prey becomes scarce.

    Climate change is another problem. For example, polar bears require sea ice to hunt sea mammals such as seals and walruses. As the planet heats up, sea ice in the Arctic is shrinking, diminishing polar bears' opportunities to hunt.

    Overhunting has put many apex predators on vulnerable or endangered lists. As humans moved into tigers' habitats, they brought domestic **livestock** such as goats and chickens. With no other available prey, tigers would eat these animals. Humans would then hunt the tigers down and destroy them.

Amur tiger

Dingoes

⭐ Humans do not always foresee the results of their actions. In Australia, dingo dogs were considered a pest. They threatened **livestock**. But when these apex predators were hunted and removed, the red fox population increased. Red foxes preyed upon many of the small native mammal species. With no dingoes to keep the foxes in check, an alarming number of small mammals began to disappear as the foxes ate them. Eventually, the dingoes were brought back, and balance was restored.

Red fox

Burmese python

- Another way humans cause problems for top predators is by introducing nonnative species into an ecosystem. This has happened in the United States, in the Florida Everglades. Burmese pythons, originally purchased as pets, were dumped here when their owners grew tired of them.

  Burmese pythons have no natural predators in Florida and their population quickly grew. Like the anaconda, these constrictor snakes coil around their prey and squeeze the life out of them. Burmese pythons now devour huge numbers of small- and medium-size mammals in the Everglades. They even go after alligators, the native top predator.

Burmese python

Mule deer

★ Bringing animals to a place where they don't belong is never a good idea—even when the animals seem harmless. About 100 years ago, people brought mule deer onto an island in California. They were brought to attract hunters to visit the island. Soon there were a lot more deer than hunters. The deer are now eating much of the plant life on the island. Many of them are starving because there are not enough plants to keep them all fed.

Great horned owls   Baby fox

- Rats, mice, gophers, moles, and other small mammals can be a pesky problem for humans. Humans will often use poisons to get rid of these animals in their homes and yards. Poisons are also widely used in agriculture, to keep rodents from eating important food crops. For many top predators, these rodent pests are often their favorite prey. The poison in the rodents' system can be passed on when they are eaten by a predator.

  Owls, cougars, bears, foxes, and many other predators are sickened or killed in what is called secondary poisoning. A certain kind of this secondary poisoning almost led to the extinction of the bald eagle before that poison was banned.

Cougar (mountain lion)   Brown bears

Grey wolf

★ Large predators can seem very scary. Fear of these animals has sometimes caused humans to try to get rid of them completely. Wolves and mountain lions were once hunted almost to extinction. Now we know that these predators are important to maintain balance in wild animal populations.

Cougar (mountain lion)

Herd of elk

- For example, when wolves were virtually eliminated in western United States, it led to an overpopulation of elk in Yellowstone National Park. The elk were overgrazing on the vegetation in the park, which led to a decline in other native animal populations. With the reintroduction of wolves to the park, there was an extremely positive effect on the ecosystem there.

  Once the wolves were back to prey on the elk, more vegetation was able to grow which created more habitats for beaver, moose, and other species. Even grizzly bears benefitted as they could now enjoy scavenging the leftovers from the wolves' kills.

Gray wolf

Moose

Beaver

Siberian tiger

Polar bear cubs

★ Humans have been called the apex predator of the entire world. But maybe we need to adjust our identity from being the top *predator* to being the top *caretaker* of the world. After all, it is the only world we have.

Hawk

Caiman

Glossary

stealth *(stelth)*
a cautious, secretive way of moving

stalk *(stawk)*
to quietly track or follow

raptor
a bird of prey

talon
a claw on a bird

immobilize *(im-MOE-bih-lize)*
to stop from moving

constrictor
type of snake that kills prey by coiling around it and squeezing until it cannot breathe

Questions to Ask After Reading

Add to the benefits of reading this book by discussing answers to these questions. Also consider discussing a few of your own questions.

1 Do you think predators are important? Why or why not?

2 What are some of the qualities that can make an animal a top predator?

3 What are some of the advantages a flying predator might have?

4 What does it mean to have a balanced ecosystem?

5 What might an ecosystem with no predators look like?

If you liked **Top Predators**, here are some other
We Both Read® books you are sure to enjoy!

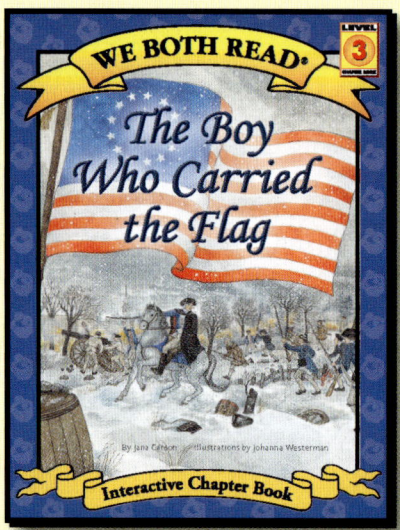
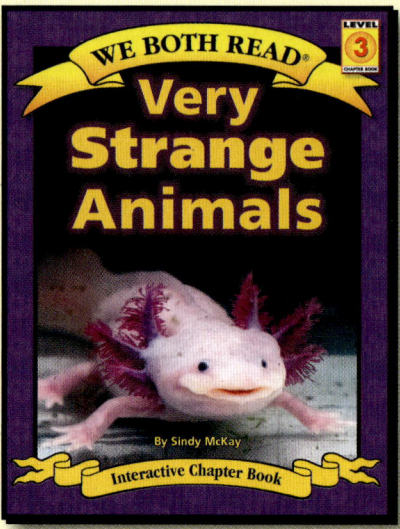

You can see all the We Both Read books that are
available at WeBothRead.com.